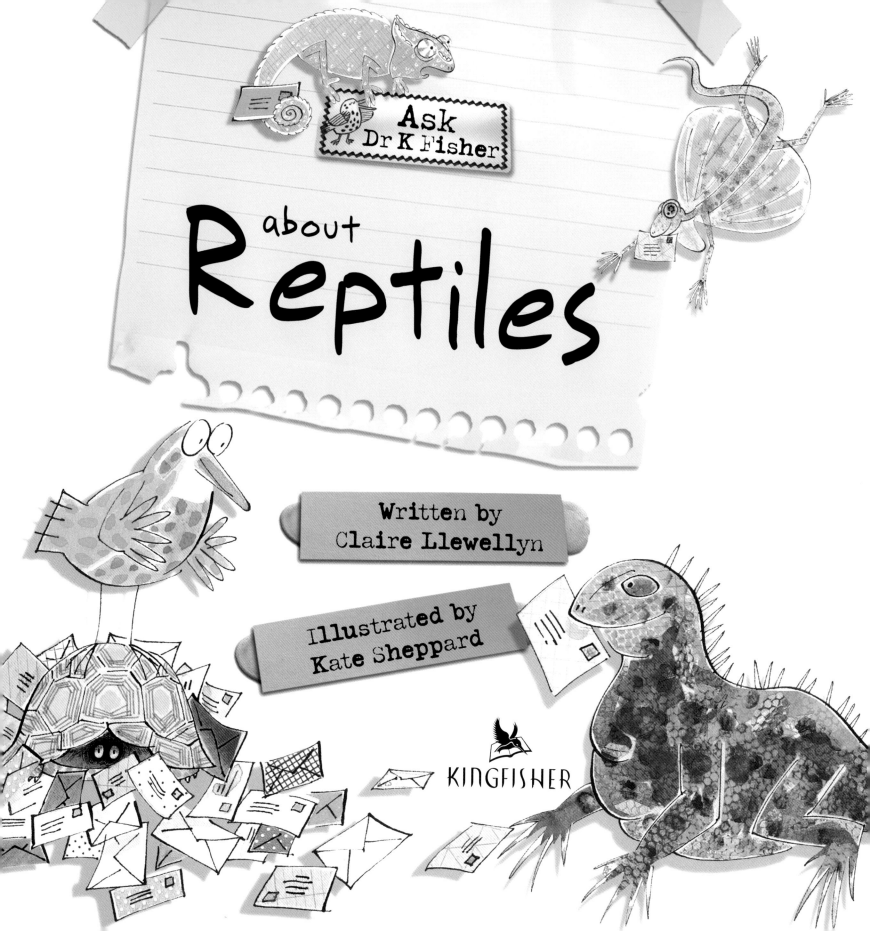

Ask
Dr K Fisher

about
Reptiles

Written by
Claire Llewellyn

Illustrated by
Kate Sheppard

KINGFISHER

**Claire**

**Kate**

KINGFISHER

First published 2008 by Kingfisher
an imprint of Macmillan Children's Books
a division of Macmillan Publishers Ltd
The Macmillan Building
4 Crinan Street
London N1 9XW
Basingstoke and Oxford
Associated companies throughout the world
www.panmacmillan.com

Consultant: David Burnie

ISBN: 978-0-7534-1575-7

9 8 7 6 5 4 3 2 1
1RD/0908/MPA/SCHOY(MPA)/157MA/C

A CIP catalogue record for this book is available from the British Library.

Printed in China

*To my friend Tali – C.L.*
*For Potae – K.S.*

Kingfisher,

Macmillan Children's Books,

4 Crinan Street,

London N1 9XW

# Ask Dr K Fisher about...

## Hot, hot, hot!

frog

Dear Dr K Fisher,
I'm an alligator and I'm a real sun worshipper. I spend hours sunbathing every day. But I know the sun is very strong. Do you think I'm over-doing it?

Sun Lover,
in the swamp

THE EVERGLADES
23RD AUG
POST

Dr K Fisher,
1 Diving-in-the-Water,
Birdsville,
KF1 1YZ

4

alligator
**warming up**

spoonbills

**Dr K Fisher**
**Any problem solved!**
1 Diving-in-the-Water,
Birdsville KF1 1YZ

Dear **Sun Lover**,

All reptiles need plenty of sun – that's because you are cold-blooded, and your body temperature changes with your surroundings. In the morning, after a long, cool night, your body feels lazy and slow – it can't even digest your food. So it's very important that you bask in the sun. As your body warms up, you have more energy. If you still feel too warm, open your mouth and let the breeze blow inside. Alternatively, move into the shade or take a dip in the cool swamp water.

Best wishes,

Dr K Fisher

cooling off!

5

# Here's a gecko that's had a shock

## A lucky escape!

Dear Dr K Fisher,

I'm a gecko and I've had a terrible accident. The other day I was attacked by a snake, which bit off my tail. I managed to escape, but I really loved that tail. Now I can't seem to face my friends without it. How will I ever get my confidence back?

Lost-my-tail,
in the tropics

tree snake

gecko

tarsiers

**Dr K Fisher**
**Any problem solved!**
1 Diving-in-the-Water,
Birdsville KF1 1YZ

Dear **Lost-my-tail,**

When predators attack a lizard like you, they often grab hold of the long, skinny tail. But they don't know about your great defence - your tail breaks off and wriggles on the ground! It's a terrific trick that surprises the predator, and gives lizards the chance to escape. I have good news for you: your tail will re-grow over the next few weeks. It may be a slightly different colour and it will contain rubbery cartilage instead of hard bone. Still,
a tail's a tail!

**Yours sincerely,**

Dr K Fisher

**New tail!**

Turn the page for **more** on **reptile defences...**

7

# Dr K Fisher's Guide to Reptile Defences

Smaller reptiles make tasty **meals** for **mammals**, birds and larger **reptiles**. But many of **them** have clever defences and could win **prizes** for **their** skills in staying alive!

TOP SURVIVOR – frilled lizard

Puffs out its neck frill to look big and scary

SURVIVAL CHAMP – grass snake

Pretends to be dead, so predators will think it's not fresh enough to eat

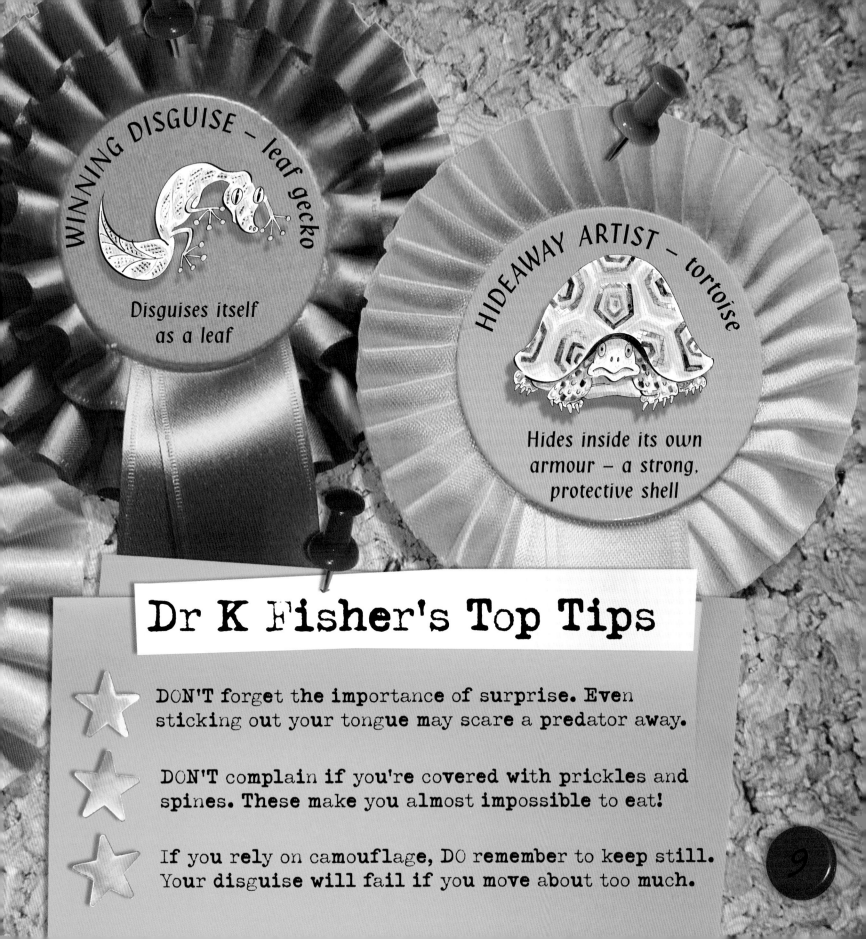

WINNING DISGUISE – leaf gecko

Disguises itself
as a leaf

HIDEAWAY ARTIST – tortoise

Hides inside its own
armour – a strong,
protective shell

# Dr K Fisher's Top Tips

DON'T forget the importance of surprise. Even sticking out your tongue may scare a predator away.

DON'T complain if you're covered with prickles and spines. These make you almost impossible to eat!

If you rely on camouflage, DO remember to keep still. Your disguise will fail if you move about too much.

# Here's a troubled rattlesnake

## A scary tale

Dear Dr K Fisher,
I'm a rattlesnake, and even though I'm one year old, I still play with the rattle at the end of my tail. My friends tell me that rattles are for babies, and snigger behind my back. But I just can't seem to break the habit. Will I ever grow up?

Snake-Rattle-and-Roll,
in the Arizona desert

diamondback rattlesnake

**Dr K Fisher**
**Any problem solved!**
1 Diving-in-the-Water,
Birdsville KF1 1YZ

Dear **Snake-Rattle-and-Roll,**

It's time to clear up a muddle: your rattle is not a babyish toy. It's an early-warning system. Your tail is made of dry, scaly rings, which buzz loudly when you give them a shake. When nearby animals hear the noise, they freeze, then move quietly away. They know you carry a deadly poison that could kill them in a trice. Rattling your tail helps you to avoid risky fights in which you could get hurt.

It also saves your precious poison for another day.

**Best regards,**

Dr K Fisher

grey fox creeping away from rattlesnake

11

## I'm so tired!

Dear Dr K Fisher,

I'm a female green turtle and every year I leave my feeding grounds and swim hundreds of kilometres to lay my eggs on a distant beach. This year, I can't face the long journey and I'm thinking about laying my eggs on a beach nearer home. The other girls say this is a bad idea. What do you think?

Want-an-Easy-Life,
in the Indian Ocean

green turtle

12

the route to the nesting site

**Dr K Fisher**
**Any problem solved!**
1 Diving-in-the-Water,
Birdsville KF1 1YZ

Dear **Want-an-Easy-Life,**

I advise you to stick with your old nesting site. Trying a new beach is very risky. Will the sand be soft enough to dig a hole? Will your eggs be safe from the tide? How will you manage to find a mate when the males will have swum to the old site? You're right, it is a long journey. If you're really tired, you could take a year off, as most turtles don't breed every year. But why waste time? Turtles are strong swimmers, and your navigation skills are second to none!

**Good luck,**

Dr K Fisher

Made it!

Turn the page for **more** on **reptile babies...**

# Dr K Fisher's Guide to Reptile Babies

Most **baby reptiles** hatch out of eggs, but some **develop inside their mother's body** and are born **live**. Only a **few kinds of baby reptiles** are looked after by a **parent. The baby cards on this page** explain about **four different reptiles.**

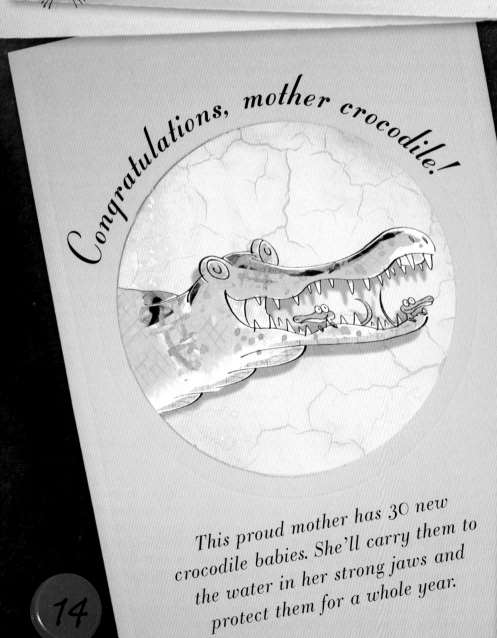

## Congratulations, mother crocodile!

This proud mother has 30 new crocodile babies. She'll carry them to the water in her strong jaws and protect them for a whole year.

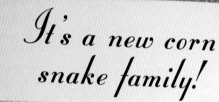

## It's a new corn snake family!

These bouncing boys and girls have just begun to hatch. They are in no hurry to leave the nest, and will stay snug inside their eggs for a day or two more.

## Announcing a safe tortoise arrival

Their mother laid her eggs in a hole in the ground. Now the baby tortoises are digging their way out, ready to make their way in the world.

## New baby sea snakes

These wriggly babies didn't hatch. Their mother gave birth to them in the sea. The plucky snakelings are ready to swim away on their own at once.

# Dr K Fisher's Top Tips

 DO **plan your family**: lay **eggs in warm soil if you want more boys**, or in cooler ground for **more girls**.

 DO **lay your eggs on dry land, never in water**.

 DON'T **worry about leaving your young. They have all the skills and instincts they need to survive**.

# Here's a lizard that wants to soar

## Up, up and away?

Dear Dr K Fisher,

I'm a flying lizard and I live in the rainforest. Every day I thank my lucky stars for my wings that help me glide through the trees. But I've noticed birds soar right up to the sky while I can only dive from tree to tree or down to the ground. How can I fly like the birds? I can't wait to loop the loop.

In a Flap,
in the forest

flying lizard

**Dr K Fisher**
Any problem solved!
1 Diving-in-the-Water,
Birdsville KF1 1YZ

Dear **In a Flap,**

I am sorry to disappoint you, but you will never be able to fly like a bird. Those 'wings' on the side of your body are only flaps of skin that spread out like a parachute as you jump from tree to tree. Unlike birds, you don't have muscles in your wings and are not strong enough to soar up into the sky. Cheer up, though – try to think of yourself as a brilliant jumper rather than a poor flier, and enjoy leaping around the forest.

**Yours sincerely,**

Dr K Fisher

17

## Toilet troubles

cactus plants

Dear Dr K Fisher,

I'm a desert tortoise and something embarrassing has happened. I was out in the sun today and (there's no nice way of saying this) I'm afraid I wet myself. Luckily, I dried off quickly, but I'm sure the other animals must have seen. I nearly died of shame! How can I make sure this never happens again?

Hanging my Head,
in the dunes

desert tortoise

kangaroo rats

**Dr K Fisher**
**Any problem solved!**
1 Diving-in-the-Water,
Birdsville KF1 1YZ

Dear **Hanging my Head**,

Don't be too hard on yourself. It is so hot in the
desert that your body can over-heat. In fact, if you
stayed out in the sun for too long, you could be baked
alive! Wetting your legs is an emergency measure that
helps you to survive. The liquid cools your body down.
This happens very rarely, so forget it if you can.
Usually, you cope well with the heat:
by resting in an underground burrow
and feeding at the coolest times of day.

**cooling off in the burrow**

**Good luck!**

Dr K Fisher

Turn the page for **more**
on **reptile** habitats...

# Dr K Fisher's Guide to Reptile Habitats

Reptiles **live** all **over the world** and **have** adapted to many **different habitats. The three reptiles** here **have special body features that make them feel** completely at **home in their chosen habitat.**

## Web-footed geckos, stand tall in the desert!

We have scaly skin that stops us drying out, and long legs that lift our bodies high above the hot sand. We can get by on very little food and water.

## Turtles, swim along and 'sea' the ocean!

Our smooth shells and strong flippers help us to swim fast. We can stay underwater for two hours at a time.

## Emerald boas, hang out in the jungle!

My green skin has bright patches, which help me hide in the sunlit leaves. I'm so strong, I can climb trees and grip branches all day.

# Dr K Fisher's Top Tips

⭐ **DO** remember that you may face danger if you leave your habitat. A turtle is not **very** safe on land.

⭐ **DON'T** worry if other animals share your habitat. You probably eat **different food** and make **different homes**.

⭐ **DO** try and **be flexible** to cope with problems. If it's too **hot**, come out at night. Too cold? Stay **underground**!

21

## What a sight!

Dear Dr K Fisher,

I'm a young marine iguana and I'm worried about my skin. It's very dry and scaly, and there are leathery warts all over my head and prickles down my spine. To cap it all, patches of skin are now beginning to peel off! What on earth is going on?

Feeling Gloomy,
in the Galápagos Islands

THE SHORELINE
16TH OCT
POST

Dr K Fisher,

1 Diving-in-the-Water,

Birdsville,

KF1 1YZ

blue-footed boobies

marine iguana

**Dr K Fisher**
**Any problem solved!**
1 Diving-in-the-Water,
Birdsville KF1 1YZ

Dear **Feeling Gloomy,**

Don't worry: your skin is perfectly normal. All reptiles have tough, dry skin with horny plates called scales that stop you drying out in the sun. Snakes have scales that are very smooth, while for tortoises the plates have fused with bone to make a solid shell. Marine iguanas swim in the sea, so your skin needs to be extra tough to protect you from the salt water and the hard rocks. As you grow, your old skin peels away, but there's always a brighter, glossier skin waiting underneath.

**Yours sincerely,**

Dr K Fisher

crab

smart
**new skin**

23

## Snake in the grass

Dear Dr K Fisher,

I'm a rat and I could do with some advice. There's a python who keeps wanting to cuddle me. I'm sure she only wants to be my friend, but the other rats tell me to stay away. I think they're just jealous of our friendship. What do you think?

Feeling Friendly,
in the hills

python

rats

24

Dr K Fisher
**Any problem solved!**
1 Diving-in-the-Water,
Birdsville KF1 1YZ

Dear **Feeling Friendly,**

Stay well away from the python. She is a powerful snake, and rats are one of her favourite foods. Pythons are constrictors, which means they kill prey by squeezing it tightly until it cannot breathe. Some other snakes kill by biting with poisonous fangs. All snakes are expert hunters with brilliant senses, and use their forked tongues to pick up the taste of their prey. The other rats are trying to save your life. Please listen to their advice.

**Take care,**

Dr K Fisher

**All snakes swallow their prey whole.**

Some snakes sniff **with** a forked tong**ue.**

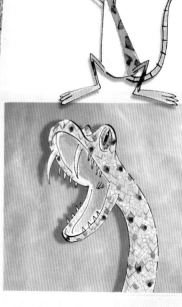

Poisonous snakes bite with fangs.

Turn the page for **more** on **reptile** food...

# Dr K Fisher's Guide to Reptile Food

What's on **the menu for reptiles**? Most of **them are** carnivores and **feed** on all sorts of animals. A few are herbivores and **prefer to feed** on plants.

## Meat-eaters

## Dinner!

*a filling feast from the grasslands*

**Nile crocodile**

**antelope**

*a tasty, high-energy meal*

**chameleon**

**grasshopper**

*delicious and can be swallowed whole*

**egg-eating snake**

**eggs**

*a fresh, fishy delight*

**gharial**

**fish**

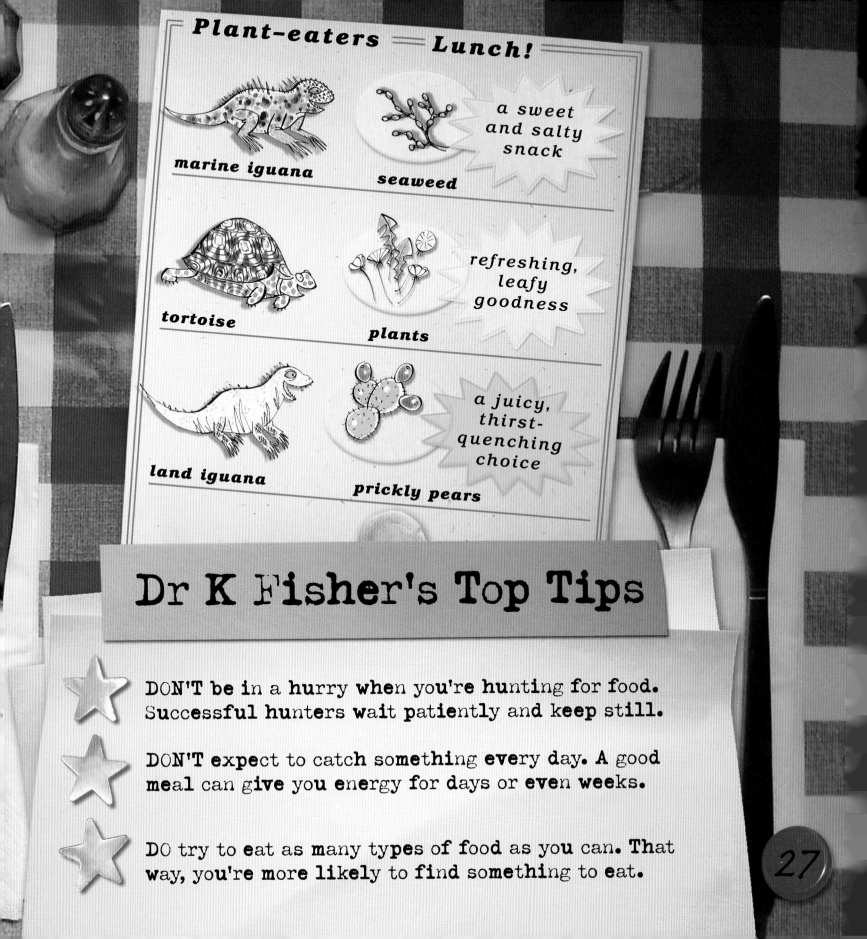

## Plant-eaters — Lunch!

**marine iguana** — **seaweed** — a sweet and salty snack

**tortoise** — **plants** — refreshing, leafy goodness

**land iguana** — **prickly pears** — a juicy, thirst-quenching choice

# Dr K Fisher's Top Tips

**DON'T** be in a hurry when you're hunting for food. Successful hunters wait patiently and keep still.

**DON'T** expect to catch something every day. A good meal can give you energy for days or even weeks.

**DO** try to eat as many types of food as you can. That way, you're more likely to find something to eat.

27

me

me again

and again

Still me!

**Who am I?**

Dear Dr K Fisher,
I'm a panther chameleon and I'm very confused. One minute, I'm green. The next, I'm yellow, or red, or white, or brown. Why does my skin change colour like this, and which is the real me?

Mixed-up,
in Madagascar

28

panther chameleon

**Dr K Fisher**
**Any problem solved!**
1 Diving-in-the-Water,
Birdsville KF1 1YZ

Dear **Mixed-up,**

Chameleons can transform their skin colour for many reasons. If you move into the sun, your skin turns pale to reflect the brighter light. If you're cold, your skin grows darker to absorb more heat from the sun. If you're angry, you flush bright red to show you are ready for a fight! Your skin cells contain grains of colour, which can be mixed in different combinations as the cells grow or shrink. Usually you're a blotchy green – perfect for hiding in the trees.

**Good luck!**

Dr K Fisher

# Glossary

**adapted**
Changed to cope with the surroundings.

**bask**
To lie in the sun in order to warm up.

**breed**
To produce babies.

**camouflage**
A shape, colour or pattern that helps an animal to hide.

**carnivore**
An animal that eats other animals.

**cartilage**
A rubbery substance in the body, also called gristle. Bones and cartilage are found in reptile skeletons.

**cell**
A tiny part of the body.

**cold-blooded**
Having blood that warms up or cools down depending on the temperature outside. Reptiles are cold-blooded.

**constrictor**
A type of snake that kills its prey by squeezing it.

**digest**
To break down food so that the body can use it.

**disguise**
A shape, colour or pattern that makes an animal look like something else to help it escape from danger.

**fang**
A special type of sharp, pointed tooth.

**flipper**
A leg that is perfectly shaped for swimming.

**habitat**
The place where an animal lives.

**herbivore**
An animal that eats plants.

**instinct**
An animal's natural knowledge of the things it needs to do to survive.

**liquid**
Something that is wet and flows easily, like water.

**mate**
To join with a partner to breed (have babies).

**moisture**
Small amounts of water.

**navigation**
Finding the way to somewhere.

**parachute**
An object, a bit like an umbrella, that helps someone to jump from a great height and to fall slowly and safely.

**predator**
An animal that hunts and kills other animals (prey) for food.

**prey**
An animal that is eaten by other animals (predators).

**rainforest**
A thick, tropical woodland. Another word for rainforest is jungle.

**reptile**
A cold-blooded animal with tough, scaly skin.

**scale**
One of the thin, protective plates that covers a reptile's skin and makes it strong and tough.

**snakeling**
A baby snake.

**temperature**
How hot or cold something is.

**transforming**
Changing.

**tropics**
Parts of the world near the Equator, where the weather is always hot.

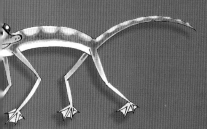

# Index